SOUNDS
ALL
AROUND

by Jane Belk Moncure
illustrated by Lois Axeman
created by The Child's World

 CHILDRENS PRESS, CHICAGO

Cover and Title Page
Designed by Dolores Hollister

Library of Congress Cataloging in Publication Data

Moncure, Jane Belk.
   Sounds all around.

   (The Five senses)
   Summary: Mentions some sounds the ear can
hear, such as the "ping" of a toaster and the
"splish-splash-plop" of raindrops.
   1. Hearing — Juvenile literature [2. Sounds—
Juvenile literature.   [1. Hearing.   2. Sound]
1. Axeman, Lois, ill.   II. Title.   III. Series:
Moncure, Jane Belk.   Five senses.
QP462.2.M66   1982   152.1'5   82-4516
1SBN 0-516-03252-6

SOUNDS
ALL
AROUND

Ears are for hearing sounds all around —
high sounds, like the alarm clock's "ding-a-ding,"

the toaster's "ping,"

the telephone's "ring-a-ling,"

or baby robins' "peep! peep!"

Ears hear low sounds too —
like the deep croaky
''chug-a-rug''
of a bull frog,

the "grurr" growl of a bear,

the "rrrr" roar of a lion in the zoo.

Now you make a low sound, too!

Ears are for hearing very fast sounds —
like the ''pop-pop-pop''
of popcorn popping,

the ''splish-splash-plop'' of raindrops dropping.

Ears are for hearing slow sounds —
like the rock-a-by rock
of someone singing
a baby to sleep,

or the ''clump-bump''
up the steps
of someone who doesn't
want to go to bed.

15

Ears are for hearing loud crowd sounds —
like a parade marching by,

or fireworks exploding
on the Fourth of July!

Ears hear soft sounds too. . .

sounds as soft as a whisper,

as soft as a tiptoe,
as soft as snow.

Some sounds are happy sounds —
like the giggles and chuckles
on a merry-go-round,

or jolly laughing clowns
doing tricks
at the circus.

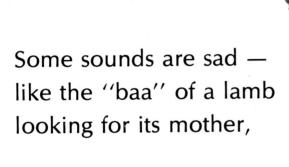

Some sounds are sad —
like the "baa" of a lamb
looking for its mother,

or the "mew" of a
little lost kitten.

Some sounds are scary —
like the ''boos,'' ''eeks,'' and ''shrieks''
on Halloween night.

Sounds can wake you up —

like a fire alarm
screeching in the night!

Sounds can make you sleepy —

like the creaky sound
of a hammock
swaying in the wind.

Ears tell you many things
even before your eyes do!

Listen to the tiny yelping cry
under the blanket. . .

and you know your birthday surprise
is a puppy!

Ears are like your very own telephone,
catching sounds from all around!